Hoodoo Voodoo I See You

is published by Kindle Direct Publishing at kdp.com,

a division of Amazon.com.

Thanks, jen

Hoodoo Voodoo
I
See
You

How
do
white
people
see
black
people
and
how
did
this
nonsense
begin?

In 1983 Wole Soyinka, Henry Lewis Gates and I developed a script for PBS, "The Image of the Black" as a working title, wherein we traced changing visions of African by Europeans and Americans over the centuries. "Hoodoo Voodoo I See You", is a text for an illuminated manuscript using video, music, photos and drama, to tell of our ancestors when forests covered northern Africa and even the Levant. Who were we when we looked at one another? And then in ancient Ethiopia and Egypt, Hellas and Rome? What did Judaism, Christianity and Islam see, and corporate slavery in Elizabethan England and America?

Volume 2 has yet to be written. Slavery in America, Democracy and Slavery.

For the script as it is today, I've learned much from Tim Whitmarsh's essay: "Black Achilles"; Donna Zuckerberg's "Not All Dead White Men"; Sarah Bond's "Whitewashing Ancient Statues: Whiteness, Racism and Color In The Ancient World"; and Professor Prudence J. Jones' ponderings of Africa at the Center for Hellenic Studies, Harvard University. And many thanks to Wole Soyinka and Henry Lewis Gates for the pleasure of working with you.

Crispin Larangeira
New York City Autumn, 2019

copyright by crispin.larangeira@gmail.com

A ballad.
Folkways Collection at the Smithsonian.
https://folkways.si.edu/classic-african-american-ballads/music-folk-blues-old-time/album/smithsonian

African and white folk in happiness and joy together. Interracial love and marriage. Noted African Americans of the social, media, music, sports and political spheres, the Obama family, for instance. The races together in church, singing and offering love to God as one.

A Happy Minister of God, (played by a Samuel Jackson in white face) turns to us from the pulpit. Cyclorama surrounding him illuminates with images as he mentions them.

                Happy Minister of God
    You'd think we have come a long way. And
    in some ways you'd be right. Here in the
    United States you can't string up an African
    and cut off his privates because a white
    woman say he looked at her. You can't just
    whip a black woman because your wife
    think you look at her with lust, even if
    you do look at her with lust. You can't
    set dogs on children because their skin
    is dark and you don't want them on
    your street or in your school. Oh it
    happen. It will always happen. I will
    not say black folk would not do the same.

             Happy Minister of God
I would not say all humans would not
do the same. I will say that's humans for
you. But you can't do it. Even if you do.
Not now, not here. But there is the human
heart.

African harming and killing African, Asian killing Asian, Hispanic killing Hispanic..

Montage. Super impose recent racial battles between white and black people, and the shouting and killing in the name of the law.

Old Lady knitting in rocking chair, (played by Samuel Jackson).

             Old Lady
Oh Lordy, that was a time and that is
a time and that will be a time. A violence
and a fear and a hate and a killing beyond
belief. And how was that and how is that?
Are we still really less than human in the
eye of so many? Are we still black devils?
And if we were not who we were seen to
be who were we and why would white
people not see us? There's most folk
today in the USA would surely claim
black and white be one under the sun,
surely claim each have his and her own

Old Lady

inalienable right to life, liberty and the pursuit of happiness. And yet there are others who would not. Others very high up it would seem. Others who will do all in their power to stop this. And why might this be so? Be it only for the almighty dollar? Well, actually and in sad truth it could be anything. Give somebody safety and immunity from the law and there's very little won't be done for whatever reason. Take away a person's rights and you take away dignity. You take away pride. You take away humanity.

Montage of humans beaten into submission from all over the world.

Image: Janiform vase with African and white together.

Nuba warrior self painting for the games.

Nuba Warrior

Once in the primal being of civilized human kind neither black nor white people saw the other as in some way not human. Oh there's those did and always will. Be they human or devil on this earth that is hard to know. But where do we begin to be different?

Contemporary celestial music, Glass, Parch, or the like.

A Massai maiden in her forest home.

>Massai Maiden
>In the beginning, everything was the same.
>Beautiful virgin mountains, rivers, trees, flowers.

And this is what we see. Then: A Neanderthal girl child, very light, almost albino and a Young Homo Sapiens Child, very black. Embraced.

>Young Girl
>At some point there were people like us.

>Young Boy
>And like us.

A montage sequence of human evolution from ape to human and the branching into separate species before joining again with the Massai Maiden.

>Young Girl
>We are from the north of Europe and Asia.

>Young Boy
>We are from the south of Africa.

Young Girl
We have light skin to catch the sun.

Young Boy
We had dark skin to reflect the sun away.

Young Girl
We have begun to explore the world. We want the sun. We want to live better.

Young Boy
Because we are human we are curious. And we have living and killing skills which allow us to survive as we travel north. In time we began to explore the world. We survive when even other species like us pass into history or oblivion. We marry them and so they become darker and more like us as we become light and more like them.

Nuba Warrior
We were hunters, and then gatherers.
Our searching led far and wide.

Now we see an early extended family huddled in a cave. We can see their fear of the dark outside, and with good reason.

                    Zulu Maiden
        At night, we huddled together, helpless in
        darkness, We feared the night above all else.

*Outside the cave. A roar of a beast, the heart rending shriek of
a human. All in the cave listen intensely.*

                    Orono Old Lady
        Darkness was the "other." The place
        of violence, fear and death.

*Early Humans staring in awe at the magnetic obelisk in Stanley
Kubrick's "2001".*

                    Orono Old Lady
        Some believe human knowing, our ability
        to know that we know and what we know
        comes to us from afar in a pillar of interstellar
        entirely indifferent cosmic consciousness.
        Let's leave that one alone. We can say
        civilizations rose throughout the world.

A composite montage of each civilization.

                    Orono Old Lady
        Mesopotamia. Egypt. India. China. Hellas. …
        You call it Greece, which, if you had any…
        At any rate, you can see it's so flattering a
        name for a people, most especially these
        people. It's more what a fat, drunk, sweaty

> Orono Old Lady
> European would do while in their masters
> of the universe period. And drinking and
> eating and stumbling while drawing maps
> of the conquered world and vomiting and
> drawing new roads around new 3D
> mountains. Talk about philosopher
> kings? These were gluttonous pigs dressed
> and ate as the old Gods did. None of this use
> the nearest sheet as the Christians do, as the
> Islam do, and the Jews. And yet they were
> Christian. They were Islam. They were Jews.
> Will I say we are different?

Montage of Slaves of every color captured by slaves of every color.

> Orono Old Lady
> People took one another as slaves. Who
> could, did. The human condition. There
> is something more to us. Sometimes, not
> often enough, we want decency and good
> for one and all. This has worked to our
> benefit.

Interior of an airplane in flight over Africa.

>Passenger
>Once you see Africa as all green
>forests in this time, you see that
>the same people lived from north
>to south and over many millennia
>those who went north got light skin
>and those went south got darker skin.
>But humanoids like Homo Sapiens
>did intermarry with hominoids like
>Neanderthals. Their descendants
>might marry one another.
>For any number of reasons, the people
>of Africa are a mosaic of color. But
>then again, so are all the people of all
>the world. No one's the same color
>as anyone else. Mind boggling.

Aircraft Captain leaving his craft after a flight.

>Aircraft Captain
>It's possible that the original humanoids
>coming from Africa may have intermarried
>with light skinned hominoid types from
>the north, making them lighter skinned.
>Given our human curiosity, our primal
>attraction to sexual scent and different
>colors, this is entirely possible.

An ancient village market, (Upper Egypt), wherein a light skinned Young Man has caught the eye of a dark skinned Daughter, a sculptor, as are her Father and Mother.

They are much darker skin than he, and clearly of a more elevated class, having done well in their business ventures. The open air shop has many fabulously colored sculptures of contemporary persons.

Beside their open lot, the High Priest of the God Amun sits in his brothel, a beautiful temple with many Young Girls of every race and color. He is quite black skin and beautiful in white linen shendyt interwoven with gold.

High Priest
You shouldn't look at her.

Young Boy
I'm sorry. I don't know what you're talking about.

High Priest
Yes you do. I'm taling about her.

Young Man
I'm not. I'm considering what to buy.

High Priest
Well why don't you go buy it.

      Young Man
I will when I'm ready.

      High Priest
And get her nose split and you a thousand
lashes. Where here you would pay your
proper respect to God.

      Young Man
Amum.

      High Priest
The highest of the high.

      Young Man
Some debate.

      High Priest
No debate. Come pay your respect to
God as you should before you make
a botch of everything.

In their open air studio the Father Mother discuss a sale with a Customer who has entered.

The Daughter colors her bust of the god Osiris wonderful deep greens and golds, very brightly and densely.

Customer
What a wonderful Osiris. You do him great honor indeed.. Splendid. What is it? Underneath?

Daughter
Bronze.

Customer
Splendid. Not cheap stone.

Father
Oh no. Never.

Mother
Wouldn't dare.

Daughter
Imagine if these were made of white stone!

They all burst into laughter.

Customer
How awful.

Father
Might as well have whites run the government too.

Again laughter. The Daughter's a bit hesitant on that one and casts a quick glance at the boy.

> Daughter
> In the beginning art is hardly ever
> white. There's the colors of our world,
> gold and green as are our rich fields
> and forests, soft hues, but very deep,
> as if a rainbow in the colors of fall.
> Reeds and seeds and flowers and
> weeds, bamboo become bowls, stone
> ore jars and swords and hoes and
> earrings, figurines, wall paintings,
> carvings, pottery, picture writing,
> mummies, medicine, science. We
> change rock and stone into temples
> and pyramids.

But now the Young Man sees a grand full body statue of Nut in all her sky blue splendor and burnished gold skin.

> Customer
> I am transfixed. Transfixed.

The Mother and Father chase after him.

The Young Man approaches the Daughter as if interested in a sale.

However, this does not go unnoticed by the Mother and Father.

Apparently, this rascal has been here before.

> Young Man
> You seem to have every god above
> and below.
>
> Daughter
> We do. Who would you like?
>
> Young Man
> I don't know. I can't decide. What do you
> think?
>
> Daughter
> But you're Osiris. Of that there's
> little doubt.

She shows a spectacular gold and green Osiris.

> Young Man
> Oh you're too kind. Really you are.
>
> Daughter
> Honestly you are. I promise.
>
> Young Man
> You find me very fertile?

                    Daughter
You are fresh.

                    Young Man
I'm sorry.

                    Daughter
You should go next door. Pay your
respects to Amum. He might be more
your type. We have a wonderful Amun.

She brings him to a wonderful full body statue of Amun in rich deep red skin, gold and greens.

                    Daughter
Imagine in your bedroom, standing
over you at night as you bless temple
virgins and yourself.

                    Young Man
Nope. Not me. I think you're right, I'm
Osiris one hundred percent. And beyond
that I love you. You know I do.

                    Daughter
…Imagine. In your living room.
Osiris.

                    Young Man
Come with me.

Daughter
I wish you wouldn't come.

Young Man
Run away. Now.

Daughter
Not now. Please?

The Young Man takes her hand.

Young Man
Don't be afraid.

They run off.

High Priest
Excuse me. I fear your daughter has
run off with that man.

The mother and father run off. The High Priest follows, but first, addressing the Customer:

High Priest
Why settle for metal and stone when
you can have flesh and blood and
serve the gods at the same time?
Please? Come.

And his Temple Maidens begin their seductions.

But now the Father and Mother enter with the Young Man in chains, held by Police, and the girl with a rope around her neck and crying hysterically.

>Father
>Cut off her nose.

>Mother
>No no, oh by God. Oh sacred Ra
>and Aten please stop him.

>Father
>Then take her. Go on. Take her to Amun.
>Let her serve Amun, if she can, if she's
>still a…

>Mother
>Oh please, won't you stop. Can't you
>stop.

She holds onto the Daughter. They fall in a heap crying.

>Father
>Do you want her? How much for her?"

>High Priest
>How can I pay for her? She's sinned.

>Father
>We don't know that.

Mother
My dear sweet innocent daughter.
Of course she is. And who do they
buy? You? They don't buy you.

Father
They don't buy you either.

Mother
She's the one they buy. She's the
only one. Do you see when she cuts
stone?

Father
...I know. She's a real artist. My dear,
I'm sorry I... I became angry. ...He's
a nice enough young man, but his
family, you see. It's not his color.
We are all the same color no matter
what color we are.

Mother
He's poor. That's the problem. His
family. And we're not rich.

The Young Man bursts in. Having broken from his captives, he's badly beaten. He looks at the Daughter. She looks at him. He runs away.

Ruins of a small Temple in ancient Alalakh. The Statue of Idrimi.

                    Statue of Idrimi
Hello, I'm the statue of Idrini, ancient ruler of Alalakh and great king of the Habiru. First of all, let me say, you understand that everything I say here has got to be visualized. You don't want everybody falling asleep. At any rate, as to Habiri, or Hebrew, and our conquest of the land of Canaan thirty five hundred years ago, you may know us as the Apiru. The dirty ones, but also the ones covered in dust, because we are laborers, bowmen, slaves and over hundreds of years we escape across forests, mountains, deserts. We come from all the lands have taken everything from us, lands you know today as Egypt, Syria, Iran, Iraq, Lebanon, Jordan, Palestine and Israel. We are tough as nails and know our way in unknown places. Skills which serve us well as we join and find we will need to agree on laws if we are not to kill one another. Such is our strength and our anger.

Statue of Idrimi
We will need someone or something
better than we to keep these laws.
There's a god some men escaped from
Egypt brought with them. Tough men,
them, fought their way out of Egypt,
crossed Sinai on foot mind you,
and their god just like them, tough
as nails, and not above charming
a lady now and then. Yahweh. That's
what they call him. We like this god.
He understands us and we understand
him. For example, how are we to eat
now that we will be killed on sight by
anyway able to do so? Yahweh says go
and take what is rightfully ours. Let the
ones who want to kill us feed us. They
have so much. We have nothing. And so
we take what we need until we are a
mighty fighting force and we take what
we want. How quickly people forget.
I united all the Habiru under me. We
came down from the mountains and
we took Canaan. We made it ours.
…You'd never know it. Look at me, I
look like a pile of dung. But if you see
me as I was. How could I be one color
if we were all together every color under
the sun?

And presto, the Statue of Idrini becomes splendid in all its original colors.

>Statue of Idrimi
>We loved each other. No matter our
>color.

Artifacts and representations of brown Moses and his African wife Zipporah. Then Moses and Zipporah in love in their tent.

The women outside, gossiping, are from light brown to very dark. Zipporah comes out.

>Zipporah
>I am black but comely, o ye daughters
>of Jerusalem, as the tents of Kedar,
>as young women of Jerusalem, I am
>dark and lovely. Do not stare
>because the sun has gazed on me.

She and Moses embrace in thunder and lightning.

Quiet Palace Garden. Sheba and Solomon.

>Sheba
>In the Hebrew Bible, Sheba tells
>Solomon "Ethiopia shall stretch
>forth her hand to God." Sheba,
>Pharaoh's daughter, will be a Jew
>and marry Solomon.

The gods, Yahweh and Yah, both brown, Yah more so, sit around a camp fire eating.

                Yahweh
Hi, there, Yahweh, the Hebrew God
of Genesis, a a man-god "J" says,
that woman some say first first wrote
down the Torah stories, but there are
so many different writings and
readings and meanings from that time
that we can never say there is only
one. We can say I'm the god of
the Habiri now. Yahweh. God of the
Habiri.

                Yah
Did you say something about an
introduction?

                Yahweh
He's Yah. Maybe an uncle of mine.

                Yah
The point is, everyone but you
knows you're from my loins as
it were.

Yahweh
Don't you have anything to do?

End of the Bronze Age. Hebron. A *Hebrew and an Egyptian Merchant. Partners. An open shop laden with the splendor of the Bronze Age.*

Partner 1
Hello. The wars for Troy go on, never ending. The sea people are strong and they've come to take Troy, destroying four thousand years of splendor we call the Bronze Age, a world of subtle colors so much like our own skin. How perfect it is to make even our own image in so beautiful a material. But life has changed now. We the Habiru must fight everyone wants our kingdom. Throughout the civilized world from Troy to the very heart of the Nile there's no stability and no peace. Jew, African, the people of the Levant and beyond into India and China, the civilized world, we had it pretty good. That's why they've come, the barbarians, because they are animals.

Partner 2
That's the problem with the north. Savages.

Partner 1
Breaking into our lands and stealing.

Partner 2
Stealing? Think rape and murder.

Partner 1
I hate seeing it.

Partner 2
"Barbarians" covered in hair. We catch them and make them slaves.

Partner 1
And of course they produce children.

Partner 2
Steady as clockwork I might add.

Partner 1
The farmers love them. Love them.

Partner 2
These small farms here, there, every where. Take away the loneliness.

Partner 1
Everyone wants more. No one is
ever satisfied.

Partner 2
Never enough. Never enough.

A Restauranteur proudly stands in his outdoor shop. His many
"Child Slaves" serve his patrons.

Merchant
I have to admit, they are really no
different than us, no matter what
their color. Some are bright. Some
are stupid. Some are so very
beautiful and… My customers
love them. Adore them.

He shows his happy Customers served by Child Slaves.

Merchant
This war between the sea people and
Troy, it is the end. I know it.

https://en.wikipedia.org/wiki/Category:Trojan_War_films

Present Ruins of Troy.

*Helen of Troy sitting on a rock. She watches Hector and
Achilles fight one another.*

Helen of Troy
Hello. I'm Helen. That's Achilles. There's
Hector. This is Troy. There was a great city
here. A bridge binding Asia and Europe.
There were many cities here, all built,
burned down over and again for a
thousand years. You could say the lands
of the Hariri, scattered here and there as
they were began almost outside our gate
and on to Sinai and the Red Sea. We had
no quarrel with them. And they did come
and fight with us against the Sea People.
Many of them. From here and there. As
was their nature.

Paris enters. They embrace.

Paris
Hello. Paris. How do you do? As with
the Hariri and other people, we Trojans
had our grand stories to guide us and tell
us who we are. Our tales of great heros
and gods were not so different were many
and long, and in time became one with the
tales of our enemies the sea people, and then
Homer's Iliad and Odyssey some eight
hundred years before Christ, just up the road
from Judea and Palestine. It's said the
daughter of Solomon, put down the old
Torah stories in the same time.

Hector
Great and grand Troy is the template for
what is seen as best in human nature. Love.
Love for another no matter our color nor
shape. And color and shape play an important
role forming who we are.

Paris
As always, our art reflects our values and
who we are. In the civilization that grows
out of the emerging post Troy world, we
are not judged by our skin, not in any racial
sense, although of course there is a growing
caste system the world over. To understand
how our art reflects our idea of who we
are, here's Professor Prudence J. Jones from
Harvard's Center for Hellenic Culture.

Montage, each image, tale, theme, Professor Jones cites is shown in various form. Strong emphasis on racial coloring.

Professor Jones
Egypt was the primary source of papyrus
in the ancient world. The first narratives
mentioning Greek contact with Africa are
in the Homeric poems, which date to the
eighth century BCE. They tell of a Bronze
Age civilization from some fifteen hundred
and more years ago. But they themselves, as
we have them, are compiled at a later date.

Imagery from "Iliad" and "Odyssey" reflecting Bronze age culture.

Professor Jones
Besides Homer, we get evidence from material culture, art, and inscriptions indicating the Egyptian Greek Minoan trade network extended to Africa as early as the Middle Kingdom almost five thousand years ago. The Dolphin Vase from Lisht, originally made in Palestine, features dolphins in the style seen in Minoan palaces on Crete. Avaris, (modern Tell el-Dab'a), temple frescoes mimic the Minoan site of Knossos. Mazes, bulls, bull-leaping, lion and leopard hunts appear in frescoes at both Knossos and Avaris. Minoans appear in Theban tomb paintings from one and one half millennia ago. Egyptian goods also appear in Greece at this time. In the Iliad and Odyssey, Homer's Ethiopians inhabit the edges of the earth, where they are in close proximity to the sun, which has darkened their skin. They are notable for their bonds with the gods. Thetis says Zeus went yesterday to Ocean to a feast with the blameless Ethiopians, and all the gods followed.

Professor Jones
Hesiod's Theogony tells of a special
bond between Ethiopians and Hellenic
gods. With Poseidon, Libya bore twin
sons, Agenor and Belus. Agenor returned
to Phoenicia and ruled there. Belus,
married Anchinoe, daughter of the Nile.
She bore him twin sons, Aegyptus and
Danaus. Belus settled Danaus in Libya
and Aegyptus in Arabia. Apollodorus (now
known as Pseudo-Apollodorus, tells us
Danaus and Aegyptus are twin brothers,
Greece (Danaus) and Egypt (Aegyptus).
Memnon, son of Eos, having armor made
by Hephaestus, comes to help the Trojans.
Jove struggles to free Io from her curse
by Hera and she becomes human again.
Now, the people who wear linen worship
her as a goddess. Epaphus, her son by
Jove, becomes king of Egypt. She has
temples everywhere. Epaphus and his
wife Cassiopeia, had a daughter named
Libya who founds a kingdom in Africa,
itself called so in honor of Abraham and
Cethura.

Throughout Greater Egypt, the Levant and Hellas, ancient and contemporary representations of sculpture, painting, architecture, stoneware and woodworking celebrate African-Egyptians and Hellenes aesthetic and sexual mores.

Sequence of Janiform vases profile both Africans and Hellenes affection. Oinochoe vase. Kantharos vases. Leda and her bull or her swan, satyrs, pan figures.

Back at Troy, Hector and Achilles sit on stones and eat sandwiches.

                    Achilles
Do we have to do this forever.

                    Hector
I think so.

                    Achilles
Doesn't make any sense.

                    Hector
Not a lot.

                    Achilles
What color am I?

                    Hector
What color are you?

                    Achilles
Some day people will really think about this.

                    Hector
About what?

     Achilles
About what color we are.

     Hector
What color are we?

     Achilles
Probably every color under the sun, given how people see what they see.

     Hector
But not white. Never white.

     Achilles
White?

     Hector
We're not white.

     Achilles
Neither is anyone else. White?

     Hector
But there is light skin and dark skin.

     Achilles
I suppose so. I hadn't really noticed.

     Hector
We don't see it at all, do we?

Achilles
Maybe a woman? Sometimes. But
for men. No. We're all brown at least,
from the sun.

Helen
If Troy is as big as poets see it, are we a
changing point in how people see each
other?

Paris
I'm not different from anyone else because
of my skin. These light skinned people are
from the north.

Helen
They aren't very civilized.

Hector
That's not because of their skin.

Achilles
Perhaps they're not very civilized, but I
treat them as I treat anyone. And for the
most part they are learning our ways. Who
knows, maybe we'll be light skinned one day.

Helen
Oh please, never, I couldn't bear it.

                    Hector
            Well, back to the salt mine.

They start fighting again

The BBC presentation: "Troy: Fall of a City" in 2018

Rome. Motion and still imagery of inter-racial society. Roman Baths. Rome. Men and women at the baths. The art and structure of the baths. Curiosity of the sexes and the races.

Roman Palace. Emperor Nero plays his cithara whilst looking at a roman panorama outside his window.

                    Emperor Nero
            Hello, Nero, here, you know, the mad
            violinist burned Rome. No violins then, a
            cithara most likely, if I played anything.
            But moving along now to gravely ponder
            how we Romans saw Africans, if we look
            at the art of a particular time, we will have
            a quite good idea as to what people thought
            and believed. Unfortunately, the art of the
            ancient and classic world, for our purposes
            Africa-Egypt, Hellas (or Greece), and Rome,
            has been severely compromised and
            misinterpreted. Here's Sarah Bond on
            what we saw when we looked at each
            other.

Sarah Bond
Although today we often romanticize
the bare marble of ancient sculpture,
most of these specimens were in fact
painted in bright shades of blue, red,
yellow, brown and many other hues.

Istanbul Archaeological Museum, room 5 - Reconstruction of the original polychromy of a Roman portrait. Scientist working in Art Lab.

Sarah Bond
Scientists study the often-minute traces
of paint, inlay and gold leaf used on
ancient statues. Digital tech restores
their original polychromy.

Scientist In Art Lab
How we color (or fail to color) classical
antiquity is often a result of our own cultural
values. Even today, the idea of a "pure, marble-
white Antiquity" prevails. Many thanks to
Johann Joachim Winckelmann for one.

Jonann Joachim Winckelmann appears, describes illustrations of his white beauty aesthetic. These include sculpture, mosaic, paintings, photos and movies. Johann becomes confused as black and white mingle. Visuals of The Apollo of Belvedere.

                    Sarah Bond
White marble was seen as the ideal of
beauty. The Apollo of the Belvedere is
itself a marble copy of a 4th century
BCE Bronze Greek original.

Visuals: Original Apollo in Bronze.

                    Sarah Bond
While many Greek sculptors used bronze,
Romans preferred the more durable marble.
They were making material decisions.

Roman Artist considering large marble cube, and large sheet of bronze. Winkelmann appears, studying a bronze statue and a white marble statue side by side. Bronze statue disappears. Visual progression from bronze to white marble.

                    Roman Artist
But Winckelmann saw ideal beauty.

                    Sarah Bond
Color in Sculpture came to mean barbarism.

Visuals/orals chronology from ancients and classical ages.

                    Roman Sculptor
We did work in different marbles for skin tone.

Range of color for marble and works of art created in that material. He might show and describe each.

> **Roman Sculptor**
> Yellow, red and black were often applied as an underpainting before painted details were added.

Female Roman Artist. She creates a piece as she speaks.

> **Female Roman Artist**
> Eyebrows, jewelry, clothing with a vibrancy white marble can not provide. To really see my work, modern restoration must undo destruction gone on for thousands of years. ...Sorry, don't mean to get so excited. But still... Really. Honestly.

Istanbul Archaeological Museum, room 5 - Reconstruction of the original polychromy of a Roman portrait. Sarah Bond Visuals shown here, not spoken.

Scientist at Istanbul Archeological Museum.

> **Scientist at Istanbul Museum**
> Ceramics from both the Hellas and Roman periods reveal a fascination with Africans and particularly Ethiopians, but they did not employ what W.E.B. Du Bois would call a "color prejudice."

Mosaics and wall paintings. Smaller vases as well, urns, jars, bowls..

Roman Arts Merchant with successful interracial couple. The middle of a sale. Sculptures of many colors.

      Roman Arts Merchant
    Romans generally differentiated people
    on their cultural and ethnic background
    rather than skin. On the other hand, when
    it came to making racist jokes, sculptors
    could be nasty.

Disfigured works by sculptors making fun of others, including Africans.

      Interracial Couple Woman
    Sarah Bond tells us Classical art could
    exaggerate facial features. But we did
    not engage in the construct of biological
    racism.

      Interracial Couple Man
    People cheated and hated each other for all
    the reasons we do so, but not for race.

Hadrian's villa. Intercourse mural, African and Roman satyrs. The Emperor Hadrian sitting in an outside shade. His Sentry near.

Emperor Hadrian
Don't mind him. The Sentry. Apparently, my life is always in danger. He's very good at what he does. Rome was... how should I put it, an extraordinary world power. Her symbols and values stretched from the Atlantic to the Ganges, the Baltic to the upper reaches of the Nile.

Roman Sentry
At first Romans admired the African much as the Hellenes had done. Here's Lactantius Placidus:

Close up of Lactantius Placidus.

Lactantius Placidus
"Certainly they (the Ethiopians) are loved by the gods because of justice. This even Homer indicates in the first book. Jupiter frequently leaves heaven and feasts with them because of their justice and the equity of their customs. The Africans are said to be the most just of men and for that reason the gods leave their abode frequently to visit them."

Theatre of Pompey. Julius Caesar. Brutus and Cassius.

Julius Caesar
Theatre of Pompey. Most interesting
building. Here's where they killed me,
those two, Brutus and Cassius. On my
way to be made Emperor for life. Gone
now. The building. You'd think they
could have saved where I died. But as
to Africans, we still got along very well.
There was difference. For instance,
Cleopatra comes from a very old
family, the Ptolemy, who are
Macedonian. But over centuries in
Egypt they did of course intermarry
with Africans. That doesn't matter.
What matters is that she's Egyptian
and now they're the enemy, just like
Carthage. But then again, we Romans
have deep roots in Egypt.

Close up of bust of Diodorus Sicilus, superimposed on sequence of Roman murals, mosaics, paintings, artifacts verifying his words.

Diodorus Sicilus
The Ethiopians conceive themselves to
be of greater antiquity than any other
nation; and it is probably that, born
under the sun's path, its warmth may
have ripened them earlier than other men.

Noble Woman and Man.

                Noble Woman
And they state that by reason of their
piety towards the deity, they manifestly
enjoy the favor of the gods, in as much
as they have never experienced the rule
of an invader.

                Noble Man
From all time they have enjoyed a state of
freedom and peace with another, and although
many and powerful rulers have made war upon
them, not one of these has succeeded.

Emperor Caracalla gets out of his bath. He brushes his teeth.

                Emperor Caracalla
Hello, Lucius Septimius Bassianus here,
African emperor of Rome. Ours is an ancient
family, with a long history in Africa. And of
course, so much of Rome has settled in my
dear old Africa, the legionnaires when they
first come and pillage and burn and rape,
and then upon retirement. Take a wife, buy
a bit of land, or marry into land.

He sits. A Roman Painter continues painting a bust of him.
Montage of sources yet to be located, identified.

Roman Painter
When doing his portraits in stone or
cloth, if it's stone I paint the stone in
color more his own. I work in sands,
tans, dark greens, browns, purples,
reds. Just like the gods. They also
get splendid color covering.

Emperor Caracalla
As to Africans and Romans, I would
say we begin to see ourselves as
different people, and there might be
some racist notions of color creeping in.
Of course I don't help. I wouldn't call it
temper, when I murdered my brother.
There was an empire in danger and we
couldn't agree for love of money or any
thing else. And the slaughters here, there,
when you think about it. I don't look good.
To them. The people. Even Africans don't
like me. It's just my way. But I'm not black
because I'm evil. The truth of the matter
is that if you are in the sun all day you
become dark, which isn't true of northern
savages, who turn beef red or chicken
pink. But in general I would say, even
with this subtle shift in how we see one
another, We're still Romans. People still
do one another in, of course, but not for
the color of their skin.

Romans settling Africa, and Romans of all race and creed together as they congregate. Panorama of classic white statues coming through original colors. Visuals and orals of artists as well as scientists bringing ancient and classic artifacts back to their original state. Resurrection.

Head of a Young Man. Centrale Montemartini, Rome, Italy. Color and gilding still visible.

>Head of Young Man
>I feel so white. I've been stripped naked.
>This isn't me. I had color. Lots of color.
>I was rich in color.

He turns a rich dark brown.

Bust of Scipio Africanus, African-Roman General.

>Scipio Africanus
>Scipio Africanus here, African Roman
>General of the Empire. You've already
>met one purveyor of stupid stinking
>lies about Africans, Winckelmann. Died
>way after me, 1768, I should think. Never
>mind that. Good riddance. Oh no. Not
>him. His loads of human bull… made
>the history of art as we know it today.

Otto, Wealthy Roman Arts Dealer

                    Otto
Hello, I'm Otto,, wealthy Roman Art
dealer. My motto's the customer is
always right. Like your Jeff Bezos in
your time. You're wondering why I'm
not a slave, right. Well, let me tell you,
I was a slave, and my mother and father
were before me. We can do very well
here in Rome, we people from the north,
Germania. They think they're better than
us, that's true, not because they are brown
or black but because they are Romans and
we are not. I let them think what they want.
Every day we Christians are stronger. Our
belief holds us together. Now, as to my
customers, they want Bronze, just to show
what real class is, I got bronze. They want
to make sure they're here forever, hey,
marble is practically free. It's all
workmanship. And what do I pay? I got
slaves. So what do we do, we take the
bronze from ohhhh, could be from any
time in history. They're all over the place
now. That's war. The ocean of fire. So, we
take the bronze and we make a copy in marble
and then we stick the patron's head on top.
We paint it beautifully. We paint it really
beautifully. Everybody's happy.

Winkelmann comes in.

>Winkelmann
>Winkelman here. I am not happy. I am not happy at all. Rome is the core of enlightened thought. This genius is perfectly reflected white marble. The embodiment of ideal beauty. Yes, my argument is somewhat circuitous, but as they say, all roads lead to Rome.

Comic montage caricature of Winkelmann as he picks objects out of the air and preaches his wares. Montage completes with rapid tempo of images in Nell Irwin Painter's: "The History of White People."

The book opens to a photo of Professor Painter.

>Nell Irwin Painer
>Winckelmann wontonly denigrated non-European nationalities. Color is barbaric.

Winkelmann slams the book shut.

>Winkelmann
>The Greeks were the very soul of classicism, They would never stoop so low as to use color in their work.

Visual/oral chronology of art according to Winkelmann.

Artist Studio. Roman Artist painting. Winkelmann sees the Roman Artist painting. He jumps about like Rumpelstiltskin.

                    Winkelmann
No no no no!

Paazza of Saint Peters in Rome. *A very dark brown Jesus crosses with his cross.*

                    Jesus
As the son of God, I preached the word
of God. A great religion was born. Maybe
the greatest.

He moves his hands as if conducting a symphony of suspended images of painted and sculpted Christs of all shape and color through the ages.

Sculpture of brown Christ on Cross in color.

                    Brown Christ on the Cross
I don't know why they thought I was
white. How could I be white? Crazy,
right? Just crazy. What people see.

A young dark brown skinned girl, Mary, breast feeds her infant in Central Park.

Mary
People say I had an immaculate
conception. As far as I know I did.
The way it began was I had a dream
Michael the Archangel came and he said
I had been chosen - don't ask me how
- to be the mother of his son, God Junior,
or Jesus as we named him. Well, You
could have knocked me over with a
feather. And then he said even
though we… God and I, would really
do it I wouldn't even know it. …Did
that mean I wouldn't feel it? You're
doing it with God but you don't even
feel it? C'mon. Anyway, I thought it best
not to say anything. Me. And I'm going to
have the son of God. "Rosemary's Baby"
I understand, but the son of God? Wow.
Anyway, I told Joe and he was tickled
pink. He said, honey, this is it, problem
solved. You know how you never let
me… you know? Now we don't have to.
We can do it the other way. So I said what
way and he said you know, the way the
priests do it.

A bedroom in Ovid's house on the Baltic. Cold Steel grey. Ovid in bed with an African Slave Girl.

Ovid
Hello, Ovid here, noted poet and in
the end exile due to corrupting the
Emperor's sister apparently, when
she read my poems. Can you imagine,
for that I am exiled to the end of the
Empire. At any rate, What are we on
about? Oh yes, racism in Rome. Well,
I can tell you we did not have racism
as you know it today. In fact, as with
the Hellenes, we Romans felt quite
the opposite.

African Slave Girl
But you see how they treat us.

Ovid
You mustn't pay them any mind,
dear, Trust me, for me and my
friends you are enchanting.

African Slave Girl
I'm telling you they don't see me as
they did. It's changing.

Ovid
Probably all to do with Africa, now
that we want to own it. Take away
humanity and you can do what you
want with someone.

>Ovid
Nothing to do with us, though. We're miserable enough I'm afraid.

>African Slave Girl
You're changing.

>Ovid
…Suppose I did love one like you.

>African Slave Girl
You never would.

>Ovid
Agamemnon fell For Phoebas; and the great Achilles gave his heart to golden Briseis.

The Scene as if in a dream. Ovid's wife enters scowling.

>Ovid (Voice Over)
But when she fixed on you her angry frown, You blushed, I saw you. I had more control, If you remember, I swore up and down that I was faithful, perjuring my soul. Venus forgive me; let the south wind sweep the lies, they were a gentleman's, and you, my dark beloved, shall we sleep Tonight, together?

Humiliated, angry, the African Slave Girl comes to the edge of the set.

                African Slave Girl
What's interesting here is not just
the sense of guilt he has for cheating
on his wife, but his discomfort because
I am African. Something has changed
in the Roman mind and for that matter
the collective human mind of classicism.
There is a knowing separation. The
African wars. We're taking everything,
including their humanity.

                Ovid
And do you include yourself as one of us
my precious one.

The African Slave Girl ponders, then enters his bed.

Light on Horace and Plutarch.

                Horace
Horace.

                Plutarch
Plutarch.

                Horace
I say watch out for the African.

> Plutarch

Couldn't agree more. Unlucky bastards.

> Horace

Not a bad sort, really, but bear the
curse of Canaan on them. Drag it in
with them.

> Plutarch

The old idea of a dark underworld,
that's where it comes from, and that's
where they come from.

> Roman Citizen

I worry about these Africans.

> Second Roman Citizen

Africans? Why they are just as we are.
Always have been.

> Roman Citizen

Rape us in our beds.

> Second Roman Citizen

You should be so lucky.

> Roman Citizen

Cut your throat on a dark night, watch
and see if it isn't so.

						Second Roman Citizen
Go on.

						Roman Citizen
Don't you say so to me. I see your
look on her more than I care say.

						Second Roman Citizen
You're carrying on for no good reason.

Wealthy Female Patron wanders an artist studio filled with works of art in color..

						Wealthy Female Patron
Actually, the truth of the matter is that
Africans were a favorite subject of pre-
Roman literature and art, especially
when it had to to do with sex. A major
theme of the endlessly adulterous Romans
was the faithless wife attempting to
seduce an African.

She sits near African Boy on a bed. Saint Judas the Apostle comes forward.

						Saint Judas the Apostle
Hello, Saint Judas here, Not that one.
The other one. Were two of us traveled
with the savior. But as to Africans and the
Curse of Noah, Canaan if you prefer.

Saint Judas the Apostle
Even I wonder sometimes. The Africans are
bad luck. We're the same color but they are
bad luck. Don't ask me why. The will of God?
The ancient biblical curse?

African Free Woman
There's nothing to wonder about. As the
empire falls, and the north has its day,
we are different. Increasingly, for Romans,
Africans are the cursed "other" because of
our skin. And let's face it, when times are
bad everyone needs somebody to kick.

Color slides of Genesis story. Noah appears in thunder and lightning. He carries an umbrella. Montage of Noah's curse of Ham.

Noah
Romans were of course aware of the
Genesis story where I condemned Ham,
my son. Whether or not true or false,
these stories had been around forever,
long before they were all knit together
into a grand tale. But they came
alive again in the late Roman empire.

Frightened Roman African Homeowner attending his garden.

>Frightened African Homeowner
But what led to the degradation of the
African? How did Romans wind up
with these ideas of who we are?

Montage of Africans and Romans as Romans ascend in their African wars.

>Caesar
When I fell that was the end of Rome.

>Cleopatra
It did go on almost five hundred years.

>Caesar
…But not the same. Not at all.

>Cleopatra
Nothing is ever the same.

>Caesar
A world in harmony with itself and the gods. Order. Glory. And empire. That's what I left. And now it's gone. Why?

>Cleopatra
For Caesar, I'm his equal. I like that about him. Actually, he thinks he's stepping up, marrying into the Ptolemy. I am more a divinity than a queen.

Cleopatra
Or better put, they were much the same.
Caesar, like most Romans, is only a man.

Caesar
A man. And then a god. That wasn't good.

Mark Anthony wanders in, wounded, and falls on his sword.

Cleopatra
Anthony. So romantic. Very Italian. It's
over. No, not Anthony and I. I won't go
on alone. They're not dragging me through
the streets. My family. We're done. We've
ruled Egypt since Alexander ruled the world,
but we're done. Octavian.

Statue of Octavian being stripped of its color until only marble white.

Octavian
In the end, Caesar's wish to be immortal,
Anthony's obsessions and Cleopatra's…
well, Cleopatra's everything, Egypt was
mine to lose and I won. It served me well
to portray Anthony with his Egyptian…
or more to my purpose African woman.
Our mortal enemy.

Mark Anthony enters. He adjusts the sword stuck through him.

####### Anthony
Long after we were gone, and so too
all the wars with Africa, Roman artists
and historians still created debased
imaginings of Africans. But it's
Octavian's propaganda machine
and their insane images of Africans
that really got racism going in Rome.

####### Octavian
My specialty, creating images that
set one against another. And Rome
loves it. The more crazy the idea,
the more they love it. You never
saw such whacky ideas about what
an African might look like.

Busts of Diodorus, Solinus, Strabo, Pliny. The epitome of wisdom. Bakshi style caricatures of them as their images.

####### Solinus
Strange things abound in Africa. The
inhabitants curse the sun at his rising,
and like-wise at his going down. They
hate the god of light. They dream not.
And they utterly abstain from all things
bearing life.

>Diodorus
The Stratophagi are ostrich-eaters; the
Acridophagi are locust-eaters; and the
Rhizophogi are root-eaters.

>Solinus
(Annoyed that Diodorus has interrupted)
The Troglodites dig themselves caves
and live by the flesh of serpents.
Being ignorant, they jabber and gnash
their speech!

>Pliny
The cousins of the Ethiopians, the
Hermantopodes, have feet resembling
tongs, upon which they move along with
a serpentine, crawling gait.

>Solinus
(incensed at being interrupted again)
The Blemys are born headless. They
have mouth and eyes in their breasts.

The others eye him with concern, incredulity, and a bit of fear.

>Strabo
Now, now, now! Calm. I must stay calm.
My heart. To see it clearly, in general,
they are defective. They go naked and
do not acknowledge God.

Solinus
Some are four footed beasts without ears! Others have three or four eyes in their heads! But their king has only one eye in his forehead.

Present day school hut in Africa. African girl student.

African Girl Student
Bizarre and crazy as images of the African became, they were not yet bound to evil. Horrors of the dark, yes. But satanic evil? For that we go to another rising empire, Christianity.

African Christian with white wife and children fleeing to Germania.

African Christian
Hello. We're an interracial Christian family heading north to Germania. She got her freedom.

White Christian Wife
The hard way I might add.

African Christian
And she bought me. But actually, when I think about it, you never did set me free.

      White Christian Wife
Not now.

      African Christian
Not now not now not now.

      White Christian Wife
Germania.

      African Christian
Our best chance is in the north.

      White Christian Wife
You have to take your chances, you never know who or what you will meet.

      African Christian
But we are Christians and we trust in our God. We keep a watchful eye for the Hebrew and black devil you can not see at night.

      White Christian Wife
Get him. Mister know-it-all.

African Bishop Saint Maurice.

      Saint Maurice
Hello, Saint Maurice here. I'm an African Christian bishop in Rome.

Saint Maurice
Those of us who achieve success, arts, military, politics, philosophy, Leo Africanus is another, we try to correct the lunatic fringe visions scholars project about us. It's not going well.

Rome. Rome's fall. Poverty, misery. Alaric.

Alaric
Hello, Alaric here, if you haven't met me before. I took Rome the first time in 408, but that's not even half true. The reason Rome fell is there was nothing left holding it up. Oh, you had people going about their business as people will do, and most living things for that, but the entire social fabric had become so corrupt that it could no longer stand.

Roman market place. African Merchant in Gold Cloth.

African Merchant
Rome's collapse leaves a power vacuum everyone wants to fill. This is still the richest city in the world. The invasions are endless. A complete breakdown of order. And our military power is gone.

Woman Merchant
Poverty and everything comes with it.
That's what you see now. These are
dangerous times.

Alaric
It's a question of who takes Rome and
keeps it, me or almost anyone from
anywhere. I say me.

African School Hut. African Girl Student.

African Girl Student
Of course, images became even more bizarre.

Bizarre imagery of every sort of devil and "other" than human.

A *Hebrew Merchant in Germania.*

Hebrew Merchant
Hello, there, I'm a Hebrew merchant in
Germania, doing my best in hard times.
Since we lost our homeland to the Romans,
I've seen a lot of the world, I can tell you.
And not necessarily from the best viewpoint.
But I have good relations going east as far
as Japan. That's right. China. India. Persia.
Arabia. So, now you find me heading
north where there's them will pay for
what I've got to sell.

                    Hebrew Merchant
Two thousand years of staying alive. I'll
need it. There's Christians now. Los of
them. They are not fond of me.

He passes a string of Slaves chained together.

                    Hebrew Merchant
Poor devils. There but for the grace of
God go I. The times are truly terrifying.
We are cut loose from… sanity.

                    White Girl in Slave Line
We are victims of extraordinary violence,
depravity. Floggings, eyes gouged, limbs
mutilated, branding, crucifixion.

Music. A Cairo Garden Courtyard for Learning. Ibn Hisham teaches a class.

                    Ibn Hisham
Hello, Ibn Hisham here, as to what I do,
I try to understand what words mean. And
I write about the Prophet. A new power has
spread through the land. You may say the
Moors and Saracens as we were then known,
or Muslims as we are now.

Migration of Muslim-Islam Civilization through 7th, 8th, 9th Centuries, emphasis of races intertwined.

Bilal Ibn Rabah
Hello, Bilal Ibn Rabah, philologist and
trusted companion of Mohammed. the
prophet. Faced with terrors of our own
in those lands where our enemies in Mecca
are strong, we are moving west, a great
wind changing the world that has been
Rome for a thousand
years. Using the same good roads they did a
thousand years before, and the Hellenes a
thousand before that.

Bilal Ibn Rabah
In a world polarized by color we see no
difference. As. you see. In my skin you
may say I'm African, and yet I am the
Prophet's most trusted friend. Strange
about Rome, they seem to have forgotten
that when they accepted everyone as
Roman they won the world.

Image construction for this section hasn't begun. Islam, of course, could be and should be an entire episode and or chapter of its own.

Sixth or seventh century monastery. A beautiful spring day. The birds sing. Gregorian chants in background or emanating from monastery.

An African Boy Monk praying with Old Monk in old cell filled with Illuminated Manuscripts.

      Old Monk
    To protect ourselves from the savage
    Islamic scourge, we Christians have
    created fortress Europe. Our light
    and wisdom come from this book
    that comes from God. Inside our
    thick walls we have closed all the
    windows and bolted all the doors.
    Nothing will come in. Nothing
    will go out. I speak the word of
    God.

      African Boy Monk
    Knowledge and beauty are in these
     books, but we don't know how to
    read them.

Outside in the cool night air...

A starving woman covered in children quickly pulls her boy child up a mountain path to a monastery on top. A row of Old Hooded Monks awaits him.

      Woman
    God is good, evil always exists
    in the world.

Sequence montage of color prints of saints and gargoyles. Montage of Adam and Eve in Paradise.

Eve in a Brothel.

>   Eve
> We have to choose between the two.

>   African Boy Monk
> Seek guidance from those who study
> God's word.

Man howling in agony as he is stretched on torture wheel.

Medieval interpretations of good and evil.

Benign, beautiful, God as Wise Old Woman.

>   Wise Old Woman
> Not to do so may have consequences.

Old African Farmer hoeing a field.

>   Old African Farmer
> Hello. Old African Farmer here. What
> did this have to do with me? Not a
> farthing far as I know. We knew there
> were "them." Strange people who
> lived elsewhere, every kind of people
> you could ever imagine.

Farmer's Wife
Looking for this, wanting that, ready
to give this. They came and went.

Seventh and eighth century African images of Europeans and what they wanted. How did that change over the years?

University of Cairo.

Modern Professor
Although aware of the Europeans, in
the African imagination they lived in
a place, and for that matter, a time, of
no relevance.

African artifacts celebrating African Gods. African kingdoms, African monarchs.

African Priest
They have their Gods. And we ours.

Town Mayor
Their civilization... And we have ours.

Queen
Ambitions. And we ours.

Old Man
In the villages and hamlets life goes on
as always.

Young girl and boy race through a hamlet to the setting sun.

Epic movies showing Saracen hordes on horseback sweeping across the world. Trumpets, horse's hoofbeats, shouts.

      Saracen Warrior
   Islam sweeps across the world from the
   Pacific to the Atlantic ocean. India. Persia.
   Palestine, Egypt, Libya, Tunisia, Algeria,
   Morocco, Spain, Italy, France and Portugal.

Defeated Spanish Soldier

      Spanish Soldier
   We are completely defeated by them.

      Italian Man
   I was face to face with an African, and
   then a sea of them on horses. What the
   devil will they do?

Fantastic imagery: Moors looting, raping, murdering, burning.

      German Woman
   I feared the African would take hold if me.
   I ran to the church.

Magnificent Gothic cathedral. Loud magnificent choral singing punctuated by hammers and saws.

Five hooded old monks frantically writing away in a medieval monastery library. They each bow when introduced.

>Managerial Level Monk
>Inspired by Romans, the good Bishop Isidore of Seville, Bartholomew Angelicus, Albertus Magnus, Sir John Mandeville, and Ranulph Higden are churning out fantastic images.

Renditions of African Satan, Adam and Eve in paradise. A montage. African as sexual threat. Montage African/Saracen/Muslim as Satan, satyrs and centaurs.

>African Satyr
>Satyrs. The hooded Moor on his frenzied horse. He's at the very door.

He smiles sadly, then opens the door to reveal the five monks still scribbling frantically.

>Second African Satyr
>The good fathers dared not stop. They needed something new. Something inspired to show the evil moor. And then it hit them.

The five hooded monks respond in unison with a tremendous "Ah!" of realization.

Beautiful, wise, white God banishing terrible black devil from heaven.

>God
>If evil and good exist in a world created
>by an all-good God, surely evil is other
>than God. God, of course, is white. And
>so evil must be black.

>African Bishop
>Hello, African Bishop here. …Well, I was
>an African bishop. But now here in Germania
>I'm… I think I'm the wrong color.

Black lusting, violent monster with horns. Loud shocking music.

>Arab Slave Trader
>Hello, I'm an Arab slave trader moving
>west with my business, which is slaves.
>What I do is I follow behind the Saracens,
>and when they captures a city I bid on the
>slaves they took, starting very low and
>slow. I have every kind of slave. Come.
>Look. You won't be disappointed. Yes,
>now that we're moving into Africa
>they are getting darker. That's fine. I'll
>sell the light ones in Africa, and the
>dark ones as we go north.

Horrifying Satan. Loud blasts, Cacophony. Music. Five Old Monks scribbling away. They suddenly rise in unison:

                Five old monks
        Satan is black and he is the prince
        of darkness. Satan is an Ethiope! He
        is an African.

Nighttime. Little Red Riding Hood walking quickly down a pitch-dark forest road. Loud, obviously frightened breathing. Pitter-patter of a young girl's footsteps.

                Little Red
        Their revelation had three far-reaching
        effects.

Sounds crashing through forest. Little Red Riding Hood (unseen) stops. Scan of forest from her P.O.V.

                Little Red
        It united all of Europe against the
        invader.

Little Red Riding Hood running, breathing faster. Thing in forest crushing closer.

                Little Red
        It explained the existence of evil in the world.

POV Sudden figure on road ahead rushing towards camera.

Little Red Riding Hood's horrified shriek. Quiet. Peace. A full moon.

An African Slave in Chains.

>African Slave
It provided a new home for me: not
Africa, not even earth, but hell.

Group of men with torches searching for a devil. A black woman burning at the stake.

>First Man
The devil often comes in the body of a
cat.

>Second Man
That is how I saw her. A black cat.

>Fourth Man
A shaggy dog. That is what I saw.

>First Man
An Ethiope! That's what she is.

>Second man
Ay, they come mainly as an Ethiope.

>Third man
And most hateful to look upon.

Fourth Man
All together black.

Fifth Man
With a great stench and hateful odor.

A woman screaming at the top of a flight of stairs in a medieval hovel and pitching down. She runs into the street.

Woman
He took me! He took me! He tried
to break my neck and cut my throat
and then he took me and when he…
he pitched me down the stairs!

She falls in a heap on the ground outside a tiny chapel. A Chubby Monk eats at a table laden with food.

Chubby Monk
The devil it was. A damned soul for
sooth. And in the shape of a black
Moor.

An African Slave Boy, intimidated by it all, stands in shadow.

Slave Boy
I dare not venture forth alone, nor in
the night. Although I am slave to a
powerful house, I am not protected.
Anyone may say I am Satan.

The White Men see the African Slave Boy.

          First Man
And what have we here?

          Second Man
Step forth. Let us have a good look
at you. Why he's very sweet. I've been
long at sea, you see.

          Third Man
Doesn't look anything like they say he
does.

Sudden montage of absurd images of Africans.

          Slave Boy
The ideas people have as to what
an African looks like still owes
much to Solinus, Strabo, Diodorus
and Ptolemy's anthropophagi.

Safiyaa Bint Huyayy in her tent.

          Safiyya Bint Huyayy
Hello, Safiyaa Bint Huyayy here, my
mother is Barra Bihn Samawal of the
Banu Kurayza, my father is Huyayy
Ibn Akhtab, chief of the Jewish Banu
Nadir.

Safiyya Bint Huyayy

I am married to the prophet, Mohammad
and continue his work. You will have
noted that our Hebrew prophets are
respected in Islam. As with Africa, and
everywhere, slavery is part of life in
Islam. I would say Islam is progressive
in its view of slavery as necessary, but
so too is the need to follow the will of
our Lord Allah. To take away the
humanity of another human is
unforgivable. And so we follow the
laws and show proper respect for
another human being. …Of course,
humans are humans and to live an ideal
life challenging for us all. Over time
we have seen a fading of the laws,
especially with the rise of the Christian
slave empire.

A Slave Market in Africa. An African Slave Trader checking his Slaves.

Slave Trader

I had a good life as a slave and now
of course I'm a Muslim and a free man.
I worked hard, bought my freedom,
and went into business for myself. I
have to say I love this business. The
feeling of power. Nothing like it.

A young white Slave Girl catches his eye. She flirts.

      Slave Trader
  I'm already in love.

He goes to the young Slave Girl. She smiles seductively.

      Slave Trader
  I don't know what it is about me.

      Slave Girl
  It's looking at his ugly face while I
  lie in a soft clean bed and not chained
  down in the mud night and day for
  every geezer wants a poke.

Moors selling slaves to Europeans. Muslim Slave Trader.

      Slave Trader
  In the end Islam collapsed on itself
  like they all do in the end, Egypt,
  Hellas, the land you call Greece
  for some unforgivable reason,
  Rome. But one thing is certain,
  people will always need slaves. And
  now more than ever with the new
  world. World trade is opening up
  and I need as many Africans as I can
  buy, beg, borrow and steal. But No
  Christians. And No Muslims.

An African Slave Trader in his open field market.

                Slave trader
My business is rounding up slaves, and
now with Islam exploding in pieces all
over the world I make a good living at
it right here in Africa. Now that the law
is in your hands, my hands, really, you
can make of it what you want. There's
no one going to say anything unless
they can back it up. I have several
roaming bands. They mainly kidnap
women for the east, young, strong,
beautiful, every color under the sun,
splendid. For the men it's the west
and the new world. And I often get
one tribe to go at another and then
buy slaves from both of them. My big
problem is that I can't get enough
slaves quickly enough.

Queen Isabela and King Fernando of Spain.

                Queen Isabela
How do you do. I'm Isabela of Spain.
He's Fernando, my husband.

                King Fernando
We chased the moor from North to South.

> Queen Isabela
And last of all, the grand prize. Granada.

> King Fernando
La Alhambra.

> Queen Isabela
After seven hundred years.

> King Fernando
Prince Boabdil we let live.

> Queen Isabela
And his mother. We put them in a little
boat and sent them to Africa.

> King Fernando
He wept and his mother said: Weep
like a woman for what you did not
hold as a man. That hurts.

Night. Stormy Sea. Prince Boabdil and his Mother in a row boat.

> Prince Boabdil
I now will go to Africa and live and
die a hero.

Mother
My son. There he is. My son. In
Europe Islam is dead. We ran with
nothing. They wanted everything.
And worse of it is we have a Jewish
banker. If they go after him?

Queen Isabela
The Jews have been administrator and
banker for Islam seven hundred years.

King Fernando
That's ours. They stole it from us.

Queen Isabela
From Spain.

King Fernando
From God.

Queen Isabela
Good point that.

King Fernando
Thank you. Thought you would like it.

Queen Isabela
The Jew will always be with Islam.
Just to add a more prosaic note.

King Fernando
I've got just the fellow. Bit of a chef.
What else? Let's see. That idiot…

Queen Isabela
Which one.

King Fernando
You know the one. The new world one,
what's his name?

Queen Isabela looks in her iphone.

Queen Isabela
Colombo. Cristobal Colombo.

King Fernando
He's back. Thinks his Jesus again.

Queen Isabela
Lock him up.

King Fernando
Again?

Queen Isabela
He's a menace. Throw away the key.

King Fernando
This is big. This new world. Very big.

>   Queen Isabela
> Oh, the Prince of Wales wants to marry
> Catherine.
>
>   King Fernando
> England has to be a friend.
>
>   Queen Isabela
> Keep the French in the middle.
>
>   King Fernando
> They won't like that.

Princess Catherine crosses with John Blanke carrying her large trunk and African Slave Girl carrying his coronet.

>   Princess Catherine
> I'm off to England to marry good
> Prince Arthur. I don't mind marrying
> him. He's quite the catch as everyone
> will certainly say.

She goes.

>   Queen Isabela
> Poor.
>
>   King Fernando
> Quite.

> Queen Isabela

Bloody.

> King Fernando

Very. But who are we to say anything.

> Queen Isabela

Our little flower flying in the wind.

> King Fernando

I like that. Poetry, that's what it is.

Prince Arthur lying in bed dying.

> Prince Arthur

Hello, Cate, you've come just in time
to marry me before I die.

> Princess Catherine

Oh Prince Henry. Oh woe am I.

King Henry sitting on a stool.

> King Henry

Hello, Cate!

> Princess Catherine

Oh, Prince Henry.

Prince Henry
Chin up, lass. Life's not so bad as that.

Princess Catherine
I'm all alone in the world, dear Prince Henry.

King Henry
King soon enough now Arthur's gone. And here you are, you're footloose and fancy free. There's still the marriage of Spain and England.

Princess Catherine
Yes, there is that.

King Henry
You will make a fine wife, Cate.

Princess Catherine
And you a very fine husband.

King Henry
And father. Sons. Cate. Sons.

Princess Catherine
So romantic. My heart's throbbing.

King Henry
Who are those strange folk with you?

Princess Catherine
My Africans. My slaves.

King Henry
He carries your dowry and she plays
the coronet?

Princess Catherine
He plays the sweetest music.

King Henry
So, civilized. We have white slaves,
really. We don't have any… well not
many anyway… African slaves. I could
use slaves from Africa. Christian won't
be slaves anymore.

Princess Catherine
We have the same problem in our
lands. Christians see themselves
as soldiers of God. They beat the
evil moors and sent them back to
the black pit.

King Henry
Interesting. Quite religious are you?
Well, there it is, then. …but what I
was saying about slaves, we're thinking
serfdom. …For Christians. They do the
same thing but they're not slaves.

　　　　　　　Princess Catherine
A fine distinction.

　　　　　　　King Henry
True. None the less. As to slaves, my
God, there's all the new world, Kate…

　　　　　　　Princess Catherine
Our new world.

　　　　　　　King Henry
Yours and mine?

　　　　　　　Princess Catherine
Spain's.

　　　　　　　King Henry
…Right. Spain's.

　　　　　　　Princess Catherine
Our dowry.

　　　　　　　King Henry
You think so?

　　　　　　　Princess Catherine
Perhaps.

>   Princess Catherine
> We have thousands of slaves, tens of
> thousands. We have too many slaves.
>
>   King Henry
> You're a godsend, Kate, that's what
> you are, a gift.
>
>   Princess Catherine
> As many as you wish. There's all of
> Africa. And the Portuguese and Jews
> will help.
>
>   King Henry
> Well, young lady, you certainly do have
> a head on your shoulders.
>
>   Princess Catherine
> I hope I can keep it. …Joke. Kidding.
>
>   King Henry
> Tell you what, if I ever get mad at
> you I'll chop off his head instead.

Shocked reaction.

>   King Henry
> …Kidding.

African slaves being unloaded in Europe. Africans in all their positions of servitude in England, France, in the times of Corneille, Racine, Moliere, Shakespeare and Cervantes.

Portuguese Slave Trader with African Slaves, Jewish Wholesale Slave Trader, Muslim Horseman and African Warrior with black Slaves.

The Portuguese Trader has white Slaves.

          Portuguese Trader
Are you out of our mind? What are you giving up? You will never see a price like this again.

          Jewish Trader
Nor will you. I can have white slaves for nothing. Next.

          Portuguese Trader
Not these.

          Jewish Trader
A Jew with Christian slaves? That's trouble. You never know when a Muslim might not take kindly to a brother in chains. Or his family. Better Africans. Much better. Ah, very nice. Very good.

            Muslim Horseman
The best.

            Jewish Trader
No scars? No wounds?

            Muslim Trader
Not a scratch. Took them sleeping. I
think he took the men first, then we
moved in.

            Jewish Trader
Took the men? How so.

            African Warrior
We beat them.

            Jewish Trader
Your own people?

            African Warrior
We don't know them. They don't speak
our language. Africans have fought one
another since the beginning of mother
earth. We have no way to know what
hell these devils bring. We let them pit
us against each other. We sell one
another to them. For nothing. We are
so many. We could stop them. But
we give ourselves to them.

Cyclorama of a slave ship's interior. Sir John Hawkins enters.

                Sir John Hawkins
Sir John Hawkins, slave trader, at your service. I'm telling you this slave business is a hell of a thing. Virginia and the new world. Wealth beyond imagining. The indians died. We came and they died. Don't ask me why. The African is a god send. Even better. Bigger. Stronger. Nothing beats him if you want brood. Mind you will have to wait your turn. Can't get them fast enough.

Saint Peter's Cathedral.

                Pope Paul III
Slavery was always a problem for the Church. We condemn slavery, but in the end who is fool enough to turn down a cathedral? This is much bigger than me. This is a new world order. It must be the hand of our dear Father.

                Emperor Charles V
Hello, Emperor Charles the Fifth here, yes, the one put his batty mumsie in a sealed room for fifty years. The learned aristocracy know the African must be free. And we do speak about it. Forcefully. Often.

Emperor Charles V
On the other hand, we are in a new
world order. That seems undeniable.
I would say we are decent with our
African slaves here in Europe, now.
They are mainly property of my class,
anyway. I can't speak to what I don't
know. And so I won't speak to the
issue of slavery elsewhere.

Slave family; man, woman and child on the selling block.

Slave Mother
Even when we are seen they did not
see us.

Color period pictures of blacks as monsters.

Slave Father
Say we're not human and then what?
There's fortunes being made, and
perhaps we're not really entirely
human after all.

Drunk, sweaty, rich and well-stuffed merchants bidd on slaves at auction. Cursing, Insulting. Magnificent opera houses, theatres, art galleries. Globe Theatre, London. Built by Slaves.

Elizabethan period pictures in color showing Genesis story of Noah's curse on his son, Ham.

Period color caricature of white woman shocked by black slave's enormous penis. Color sequence of images, Africans as sexually threatening. An English High Church Minister.

Minister
Foul, ugly, Aeithop" with a "propagator"
that offends our Father.

William Shakespeare in bed with Christopher Marlowe.

Shakespeare
Hello, William Shakespeare here.
Christopher Marlowe there. Marlowe,
say hello.

Marlowe
Hello.

Shakespeare
Far as Africans are concerned, for me,
for Marlowe here, for most people we
know this side of the river…

Marlowe
The wrong side of the river,

Shakespeare
We see Africans as humans, isn't that
right, Marlowe.

Marlowe
Perhaps a curse of some sort.

Shakespeare
Right. Cursed before birth. But I would
say for most people even now, the
African is base and he is base because
he is overly sexually endowed.

Marlowe
He certainly is. Yum.

Shakespeare
Only high intellectual discourse with
Marlowe.

Marlowe
Oh my God! It's an African!

Shakespeare
Drama Queen. Does know how to
write a play. Better than me I hate
to say.

Renaissance Elizabethan art works depicting Africans as slaves serving whites. Color stills of Renaissance and Elizabethan country outdoor stages and theatres showing full range of black characters in plays.

Ben Jonson has been listening.

           Ben Jonson
We're taking their humanity, the way we
speak of them.

           Shakespeare
Ah, Ben.

           Marlowe
Ben Jonson. Did the first English Dictionary.
Half the words are mine.

           Shakespeare
Mine.

           Marlowe
You wrote the plays?

           Shakespeare
We all wrote the plays. They must have
an author and it can't be you. You're dead.

           Marlowe
All right, don't go on about it.

           Ben Jonson
What's it matter who's name sits on them?
What we do is show the world what a human is.
If we don't, you wind up the shit Rowley writes.

                        Marlowe
        Rowley.

                        Shakespeare
        Rowley.

*Elizabethan Theatre: William Rowley's "All's Lost By Lust"
presented.*

                        Moor
        Thou mutable piece of nature, dost thou
        fly me!?

                        Jacinta
        Th'art frightful to me.

                        Moor
        I shall be more frightful, If thou repel a
        professor arme of love, There will rebound
        a hate blacker in Act Than in similitude;
        forget me not. Have not I chassed thy
        wronger from his ground, And my
        triumphant self thy conqueror? I am
        thy king.

                        Jacinta
        I'll fear thee then.

                        Moor
        Not love me?

Moor finding Julianus and Jacinta embraced.

> Jacinta
> Base African! Thine insides blacker
> than thy sooty skin!

> Moor
> *(to Soldiers, points to Julianus)*
> Bring forth that traitor, seze that lustful
> whore!

> Julianus
> What wilt thou monster? Anything that's
> monstrous.

> Moor
> Pluck out his eyes, and her exclaiming
> tongue.

> Shakespeare
> Rowley's a hack. We all know it.

> Ben Jonson
> The way we see an African today, he's
> not only other than white people, he's not
> himself either. He might look like a man
> but inside there's a monster.

An African Slave Girl enters.

Ben Jonson
That's jealousy. But something else, that fear of sexual vitality. It's in the mind, of course.

An attractive White Man comes to the African Slave Girl and kisses her. His Wife enters in a rage.

Ben Jonson
Observation tells me white women feel they can not compete with the African woman. But our creations of African women are superficial. Take Zanthia in Beaumont and Fletcher's Knights of Malta.

Marlowe
The problem is an aesthetic one. In creating the African something other than human these writers and artists take away the possible truth of a human being.

Ben Johson
Exactly. Take this scene from "The Knights of Malta".

Montferrat

Oh my Zanthia, My pearl, I much
repent All my neglects; let me Embrace
my black cloud. Thou art more soft
And full of dalliance than the fairest,
And far more loving.

Zanthia

Ay, you say so now, But like a property,
when I have served Your turns, you'll
cast me off, or hang me up for a sign
somewhere.

Montferrat

May my life then forsake me, Or,
from my expected bliss, be cast to
hell! Oh my black swan, silkier than
cygnet's plush Breath'd like curl'd
Zephryus' cooling lemon-trees
I vow by Heaven Malta I'll leave;
And in some other country Zanthia
make My wife, and my best fortune.

(They kiss.)

Monferrat, Xanthia, Rocca

Montferrat

No lady?

Rocca
No, sir. This pie has been cut before

Zanthia
Either the devil Must do these tricks…

Montferrat
Oh thou, damned one! Worse! Thou black swoln pitchy cloud of all my affections, Thou night-hag, gotten when the bright moon Suffer'd, Thou hell itself confined in flesh,This sword shall cut thee into a thousand pieces, A sacrifice to thy black sire, the devil!

Ben Jonson
As with her mate, the African woman is not to be trusted. She too is not who she seems to be and a danger to whites.

Shakespeare
Othello?

Marlowe
Othello has heart. He's real and yet so out of his depth.

Shakespeare
He starts off well enough.

Ben Jonson
But he can't handle the complexity of modern day life. He's the old world.

Live action sequence of Othello, Duke, Brabantio, Nobles.

Marlowe
He starts off able to hold his own.

Othello
Justly to your grave ears I'll present, How I did thrive in this fair lady's love, And she in mine.
Her father loved me; oft invited me; Still questioned me the story of my life From year to year, the battle sieges, fortune That I passed… Wherein I spoke of most disastrous chances Of being taken by the insolent foe And sold to slavery, of my redemption thence, And portance in my travel's history. Wherein of anters vast and deserts idle, Rough quarries, rocks and hills whose heads Touch heaven, And of the cannibals that each other eat, The anthropophagi, and men whose heads Grew beneath their shoulder. These things to hear would Desdemona seriously incline…

Ben Jonson
But it's all down hill. Even you create
the Africans as monsters.

Shakespeare
But we don't lose his humanity. That's why
it works. His tragedy as a human, not an
African.

Marlowe
Oh the other hand, how do we know our
audience will feel as we do.

Ben Jonson
They won't.

Darkness. Screen entirely black.

Othello, Desdemona, bedroom death scene.

Othello
O perjured woman! Thou dost stone
my heart, And mak'st me call what
I intend to do A murder, which I
thought a sacrifice. Out, Strumpet!

Desdemona
O, banish me my lord, but kill me not.

Othello
Down, Strumpet!

Desdemona
Kill me tomorrow; let me live tonight.

Othello
Nay! An you strive!

Desdemona
But half an hour!

Othello
Being done there is no pause.

Desdemona
But while I say one prayer.

Othello
It is too late.

He smothers her.

Desdemona
O Lord, Lord, Lord.

Othello
How should I do this? Do you want
me to bend you all the way back?

                    Desdemona
Not all the way back. Then they can't
see me.

                    Othello
Oh, sorry.

                    Desdemona
Try this.

They rehearse a different position. Shakespeare walks in.

                    Shakespeare
We'll let them sort it out. But you can
see the African - Othello - change from
man of honor to murderous, stupid not
quite human.

And now others rush in. Shakespeare gets out of their way.

                    Othello
Behold! I have a weapon. O vain boast!
Who can control his fate. Tis not so
now. Here is my journey's end…

                    Lodovico
O thou Othello that was so good, Fallen
in the practice of a damn'd slave, What
shall be said to thee?

Othello
When you shall these unlucky deeds
relate, Speak of me as I am, nothing
extenuate, Nor set down naught in
malice. Then must you speak Of one
that loved not wisely, but too well;
Of one not easily jealous; but being
wrought, Perplexed in the extreme;
Of one who like the base Judean
threw a pearl away richer than all
his tribe.

Marlowe
You see that bit where the moor does
himself in, there's a turning point in
how we see Africans. The moor, the
African, is still human, still someone
to respect, but at one and the same
time you can not trust him. He is
not quite right. He can go seriously
wrong. The moor, the African, the
black, is no longer one of us.

Tower of London, Sir Walter Raleigh

Sir Walter Raleigh
Hello, Sir Walter Raleigh here. That's
right, made me a bloody knight. Slave
Trader and founder of the Virginia
colony in America.

Sir Walter Raleigh
Two hundred million, that's what some say is the final number of slaves taken from Africa. And I started it all. Yes, I know, Al Gore invented the internet. But I did begin it all. Lot of good it did me. I'm to have my head chopped off.

King Charles
King Charles here. I don't want to chop his head off. He's my man in America. Without him I don't know if we can hold on. I have no choice. The Spanish demand it. I can't fight them now. Slaves. We need African slaves.

Pocahontas enters played by Elizabeth Warren.

Pocahontas
Hello, I'm Pocahontas. When they came we all died. We did not know it at the time, but we lacked the necessary immunity especially against smallpox. But they still needed humans to work.

Walter Raleigh

That's my gal. …Not like that… I mean, I get #MeToo. I mean, ah, the hell with it, I mean when we first brought the Africans, they were indentured. They were just like white or brown or whatever color you like slaves who could buy their freedom. Try to make your fortune with that deal. Especially when you're talking millions. Humans, I mean. Give everyone that deal and who would you be? Haven't thought on that one, have you? And once you had people believed they were Christians, and why wouldn't they if by law they could not be a slave, once notions of freedom and human dignity spilled down into the masses. … Bloody good thing Africans knew no English. They would come to me, begging audience, having at last found some poor beggar could make their chatter into a civilized tongue, "Sir, I am a prince," and indeed you are, sir, a very prince of a lad, next. And off he'd go into America. "Sir, I am a princess." Oh you are, yes you are. You're special all right. You want to want right over there. I'll tend you on my own.

Reverend Robert Hunt, Anglican Pastor of Jamestown Church, Jamestown.

Reverend Hunt
We try, we religious leaders in the south,
to preserve some rights for Africans, but
we are overwhelmed by the need of others.

John Puritan
In New England we hate the heathen ways
of Raleigh and his colony in Virginia.
We came for religious freedom and want
peace with the savage heathens. And so we
too have need of more… Africans, even if
Christianized. And so we must sin and take
on slaves even though we do not wish to
do so. Whether or not our dear Father in
Heaven understands, we do fervently pray
and do try in every way to hear his will.

Slave ship. Slaves cramped in the horror it was.

Slave Boy
I am in the hole. It is always the hole. Hot.
Hot you can't breathe hot. Rot. Sick. Shit.
Vomit. Rats. Fleas. Dengue. Maggot.
Malaria. Worm living in you. Men.
Woman. Children.

Slave Girl
Sometimes we free ourselves and run into the sea.

Slave Boy
The sharks know this and so they follow. Every day there is more food than they can eat.

Slave Girl
The boat gets lighter. It floats high in the water.

Africa. African warriors with captured Men, Women, Children.

African Warrior
Look at this. We took them sleeping. So easy you won't believe it. They took us last year, but here we are. There's good money here.

Slave ship hole. Slave Boy.

Slave Boy
Sometimes our mothers and fathers kill us with their chains.

Slave Girl
Sometimes all the chain will rise and run into the sea.

                    Slave Boy
            Sometimes for this and for that the
            captain will chain us to the anchor and
            pull us into the sea.

Slave Ship Captain's Walk. White Cabin Boy.

                    Cabin Boy
            Ocean waters churned foamy white by
            sharks, then red with blood. I did see it.

                        Shark
            The shipping lanes became shark infested.

17th century slaves on land bowing at master's feet. Slaves carrying master to church. 18th century, slaves being whipped. 19th century, slaves being sold on block.

African woman being seduced by white man. African man running frantically through Savannas. Dogs in pursuit.

                    Dog In Pursuit
            Among those who reached the land of
            promise many tried to escape.

Shotgun blast. Slave barracks (interior) on plantation. Many families together, protecting, helping, sense of communal struggle to survive. Sad spiritual, carry sound forward and expand as: Beautiful southern mansion with slaves sowing crops. African slaves working long and hard.

Stupendous, bombastic music. Great cities rise. Ports, roads, warehouses, buildings, ships being built by Africans.

Present time. African American family at home, fireplace aglow, windows look out to trees.

Daughter studies on rug: a picture of George Washington and his slaves on her ipad.

                Daughter
George Washington and his slaves. All living together happy as could be.

                Mother
In America at its best this meant treating a slave much as you might a valued animal or even a beloved pet.

                Father
That was soon to change with the French Revolution and a growing sense in the world that all people should be equal.

                Daughter
How can you be a Christian and have a slave? I still don't get that one.

                Mother
It's human nature, I think. We all want a pet.

Father
Oh, c'mon, it's not so bad as all that.

Mother
It's true. First we sacrifice humans to
our God. But when we move away from
the cave and into the kitchen, we sacrifice
animals and now in the living room, we
sacrifice cookies and grape juice.

Daughter
I get it. In the cave humans were our pets,
and in the kitchen they were our slaves,
and now here we are.

A robot enters with tea and cookies. It serves with pleasantries.

Father
We persuade ourselves our Lord wants
us to civilize them. The Africans. That's
what they did. …To us.

Father
Even so, with cries of freedom everywhere,
we had to make clear that the African was
not really a human.

Daughter
People did that. Even then. You mean like
Racists and Rednecks.

Mother
Oh you had a very lively bunch, very
lively indeed.

Round Table Discussion. Montesqieu, F. Hegel, D. Hume, Voltaire, Abbe Gregoire, De Suray, Chairman seated around a round table In Hall of Mirrors at Versailles.

Loud circus fan fare music as characters spring to noisy argumentative life. Chairman banging the table with his hand.

Silence.

Chairman
David Hume, the great philosopher
from Edinburgh, Scotland has the floor.

David Hume
I suspect the negroes to be naturally
inferior to whites.

The Abbe Gregoire leaps up, clutching a sheaf of notes.

Chairman
The Abbe Gregoire, of France appears
to have the floor.

Abbe Gregoire
I call attention of the learned speaker
to the achievements of the following
men of color... Francis Williams, of
Jamaica, professor at Cambridge Uni...

David Hume
Indeed! But tis likely he is admired
for very slender accomplishments, like
a parrot who speaks a few words plainly.

Loud applause. Chairman Banging desk

Chairman
Le Baron Montesquieu

Montesquieu
The peoples of Europe, having
exterminated those of America, had to
enslave those of Africa... It is impossible
for us to suppose that those people are
men, because if we supposed them to
be men, we would begin to believe
that we ourselves are not Christians.

Uproar. Loud booing. Raspberries. Montesquieu, unable to continue, sits down disdainfully.

Chairman
The doctor Friedrich Hegel!

Hegel

The negroes indulge that perfect contempt for humanity!
A characteristic fact in reference to the negroes is slavery. Negroes are enslaved by Europeans and sold to America. Bad as this may be, their lot in their own land is even worse, since they have not yet attained a consciousness of freedom, and consequently sink down to a mere thing, an object of no value.

Loud applause.

Chairman

Merci, merci messieurs. I now give the floor to Monsieur Rousselot de Surgy, natural scientist.

Rosselot De Surgy

There is no reasoning in the blacks, no mind, no aptitude for any sort of abstract study. An intelligence, which appears to be beneath that of the elephant, is sole guide of their actions. One would be tempted to believe that the blacks form a gradation of humanity. from which nature seems to climb upwards, from the Orangoutangs to man.

Applause.

                    Chairman
And now ladies and gentleman, I present to you, Voltaire.

Much fanfare. Voltaire enters.

                    Voltaire.
Our wise men have said that man was
created in the image of God. Now here
is a lovely image of the divine maker,
a flat and black nose with little or
hardly any intelligence!

Loud applause suddenly cut short as: American print and motion caricatures of Africans. Early Afro-American church. A choir singing. Afro-American Preacher. Afro-American choir of Young Girls crooning behind him. White master or preacher chasing an evil spirit from a possessed black girl "House Negros" mimicking their masters life style. Playing instruments.

White master seducing an African married Woman. African Man in background, angry, helpless. The African Woman looks at her husband.

                    Black Man
There were other needs.

> Master
> What do I feel when I take her? An ancient taboo? Fear of God? Not likely. The way they look at me.

The Master's Wife enters. She hates the Black Wife. The Master's Wife angrily calls Master in.

Camera angles up to heavens.

Cut to: Barack and Michelle Obama at home.

> Barack
> Hi. Barack here.

> Michelle
> Hi. Michelle.

> Barack
> That's it for Part One.

> Michelle
> If you'd like to see more?

> Barack
> How we get from A to B.

> Michelle
> There to here.

Barack
Part Two.

Michelle
Let us know.

Barack
Let everybody know.

Michelle
Yes, we can.

End of Part One

If you have interest in helping develop this project please contact Crispin Larangeira at the email below.

copyright by crispin.larangeira@gmail.com

www.ingramcontent.com/pod-product-compliance
Lightning Source LLC
Chambersburg PA
CBHW030712220526
45463CB00005B/2015